Victorian Flowers

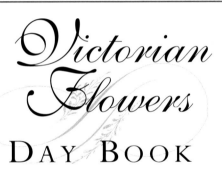

Day Book

A DATELESS DIARY IN A
CHARMING THEME

Victorian Flowers

DAY BOOK

A DATELESS DIARY IN A
CHARMING THEME

LORENZ BOOKS

This edition first published in 1998 by Lorenz Books
27 West 20th Street, New York, NY 10011

Lorenz Books are available for bulk purchase for sales promotion and for premium use. For details write or call the manager of special sales,
LORENZ BOOKS, 27 West 20th Street, New York, NY 10011; (800) 354-9657

Lorenz Books is an imprint of
Anness Publishing Limited

ISBN 1 85967 648 0

Publisher: Joanna Lorenz
Editorial Manager: Joanne Rippin
Designer: Andrew Heath

Printed and bound in China

1 3 5 7 9 10 8 6 4 2

I M P O R T A N T D A T E S

January

February

March

April

May

June

July

August

September

October

November

December

"BALLAD"

---

*I*t was not in the winter
Our loving lot was cast!
It was the time of roses,
We plucked them as we passed!

That churlish season never frowned
On early lovers yet!
Oh no – the world was newly crowned
With flowers, when first we met.

'Twas twilight, and I bade you go,
But still you held me fast;
It was the time of roses,
We plucked them as we passed!

What else could peer my glowing cheek
That tears began to stud?
And when I asked the like of love
You snatched a damask bud,

And oped it to the dainty core
Still glowing to the last;
It was the time of roses,
We plucked them as we passed!

THOMAS HOOD (1799–1845)

1

2

3

4

5

6

7

8

9

10

11

12

13

14

15

16

17

And 'tis my faith that
every flower
Enjoys the air
it breathes.

FROM *LINES WRITTEN IN*
EARLY SPRING
BY WILLIAM WORDSWORTH
(1770-1850)

22

23

24

25

18

26

19

27

20

28

30

21

29

31

Shed no tear – O, shed no tear!
The flowers will
bloom another year.
Weep no more!
O, weep no more!

FROM *FAERY BIRD'S SONG*
BY JOHN KEATS
(1795-1821)

CLEMATIS
CLEMATIS

Mental beauty

Tis customary as we part
A trinket — to confer —
It helps to stimulate the faith
— When lovers be afar —

'Tis various — as the various taste —
Clematis — journeying far —
Presents me with a single Curl
Of her Electric Hair —

EMILY DICKINSON (1830-86)

First and chief among such climbers comes the clematis. The name originally meant merely a branch of a vine, but afterwards was extended as a name for almost all climbing plants. Pliny included several such under the name; Gerard says that clematis is "a certain genericke name to all woody winding plants, having certaine affinitie because of the spreading branching and semblance of the vine"; and Parkinson has a chapter headed, "Clematis, Clamberers and Creepers," and the chapter begins with the periwinkle and ends with the passion-flower. Of the true clematis we have one beautiful representative in the traveller's joy (*C. vitalba*), "decking and adorning waies and hedges, where people travel, and thereupon I have named it traveller's joy," says Gerard; and his name has clung to it, though it has not supplanted the older name of "ladies' bower," or "virgin's bower," the last name having been given to it in honour of Queen Elizabeth.

FROM *IN A GLOUCESTERSHIRE GARDEN* BY CANON ELLACOMBE (1822-1916)

1

2

Daisies, those pearled
Arcturi of the earth,
The constellated flower
that never sets.

FROM *THE QUESTION*
BY PERCY BYSSE SHELLEY
(1792-1822)

3

4

5

6

7

8

9

10

11

12

13

14

15

16

17

18

19

20

21

22

23

24

25

26

27

28

29

Garlands for Queens, maybe
— Laurels — for rare degree
Of soul or sword.
Ah — but remembering me —
Ah — but remembering thee —
Nature in chivalry —
Nature in charity —
Nature in equity —
The Rose ordained!

EMILY DICKINSON
(1830-1886)

"Here is a new kind of rose, which I found this morning in the garden," said she, choosing a small crimson one from among the flowers in the vase. "There will be but five or six on the bush this season. This is the most perfect of them all; not a speck of blight or mildew on it. And how sweet it is! – sweet like no other rose! One can never forget that scent!"

"Ah! – let me see! – let me hold it!" cried the guest, eagerly seizing the flower, which, by the spell peculiar to remembered odors, brought innumerable associations along with the fragrance that it exhaled. "Thank you! This has done me good. I remember how I used to prize this flower, – long ago, I suppose, very long ago! – or was it only yesterday? It makes me feel young again…"

FROM *The House of the Seven Gables* by

Nathaniel Hawthorne (1804–64)

5

6

8

9

10

11

12

1

2

3

4

*C*ame the Spring with
all its splendour,
All its birds and all
its blossoms
All its flowers, and leaves
and grasses.

FROM *THE SONG OF HIAWATHA*
BY HENRY WADSWORTH
LONGFELLOW
(1807-1882)

7

13

14

15

16

17

Like Breath from heaven's
own portals
Come Roses bright
to mortals;
The Graces sound
their praises:
The Loves in flow'ry mazes
Each one, his voice upraises,
To Sing with joy Cithera's toy.

ODE 51, DEDICATED TO
THE ROSE
BY ANACREON
(C. 580-490 BC)

18

19

20

21

22

23

24

25

26

27

28

29

30

31

SCARLET POPPY

Fantastic extravagance

In Flanders fields the poppies blow
Between the crosses, row on row,
That mark our place; and in the sky
The larks, still bravely singing, fly
Scarce heard amid the guns below.

We are the Dead. Short days ago
We lived, felt dawn, saw sunset glow,
Loved and were loved, and now we lie
In Flanders fields.

Take up our quarrel with the foe:
To you from failing hands we throw
The torch; be yours to hold it high.
If ye break faith with us who die
We shall not sleep, though poppies grow
In Flanders fields.

JOHN McCRAE (1872-1918)

WHITE POPPY

Sleep, My bane, My antidote

Little brown seed, oh! little brown brother,
What kind of flower will you be?
I'll be a poppy – all white, like my mother;
Do be a poppy, like me.

What! you're a sunflower? How I shall miss you
When you're grown golden and high!
But I shall send all the bees up to kiss you;
Little brown brother, good-bye.

ANON.

1

2

3

4

5

6

7

8

9

10

11

12

13

14

15

16

*F*air daffodils, we weep
to see
You haste away so soon:
As yet the early-rising sun
Has not attained his noon.

To Daffodils
by Robert Herrick
(1591-1674)

21

22

23

24

25

26

17

18

19

20

27

28

29

30

$\mathcal{T}$he cowslip is a country
wench,
The violet is a nun;
But I will woo the dainty rose,
The queen of everyone.

THOMAS HOOD
(1799-1845)

We may add that the fortunate possessor of a Herb-garden finds it an ideal refuge for any of the odds and ends of plants that interest him… Here, too, we may enjoy such old-fashioned Roses as were valued for their sweetness, and are banished in these days, when, owing a good deal to the demands of Flower-shows, size, form, and colour are put before fragrance. Who is going to make a pound of pot-pourri (worth having) out of a whole tentful of fashionable Roses? In the herb-garden we would have the Moss-Rose, the Damask-Rose, and the Cabbage-

Rose. The Cabbage-Rose makes the best rose-water, and the Wild-briar, or Dog-Rose, is one of the most valuable for its curative qualities… And why should we not have Sweetbriar? If we do, we must remember it hates formality and confinement. Give it the wildest and most open place.

FROM *THE HERB-GARDEN* (1911) BY

FRANCES BARDSWELL

In the last month of May
I made her posies;
I heard her often say
That she loved roses.

PHILLIDA FLOUTS ME
ANON.
(SIXTEENTH CENTURY)

5

6

7

8

9

1

2

3

4

10

11

12

13

14

15

16

17

18

19

20

21

22

23

24

25

26

27

28

29

30

31

Such a starved bank
of moss
Till that May morn,
Blue ran the flash across:
Violets were born!

FROM
THE TWO POETS OF CROISIC
BY ROBERT BROWNING
(1812-1889)

"JUNE"

*J*une. Mine is the Month of Roses; yes and mine
The Month of Marriages! All pleasant sights
And scents, the fragrance of the blossoming vine,
The foliage of the valleys and the heights.
Mine are the longest days, the loveliest nights;
The mower's scythe makes music to my ear;
I am the mother of all dear delights;
I am the fairest daughter of the year.

HENRY WADSWORTH
LONGFELLOW (1807–82)

"A White Rose"

The red rose whispers of passion,
And the white rose breathes of love;
O, the red rose is a falcon,
And the white rose is a dove.

But I send you a cream-white rosebud
With a flush on its petal tips;
For the love that is purest and sweetest
Has a kiss of desire on the lips.

John Boyle O'Reilly (1844–90)

1

2

3

4

5

6

7

8

9

10

11

12

13

14

15

*S*ummer set lip to
earth's bosom bare,
And left the flushed print
in a poppy there.

FROM *THE POPPY*
BY FRANCIS THOMPSON
(1859-1907)

16

17

*Y*ou'll love me yet! –
and I can tarry
Your love's protracted
growing:
June reared that bunch
of flowers you carry,
From seeds of April's
sowing.

FROM *PIPPA PASSES*,
PART III, *EVENING*
BY ROBERT BROWNING
(1812-1889)

20

21

22

23

24

25

18

19

26

27

28

29

30

BELLFLOWER

Constancy

Great clusters of campanulas hang from all the ledges, giving to the rocks a peculiarly home-like appearance…though closely resembling the slender bluebell, that springs elastic from the airy tread of the Scottish maiden on the Highland bank, it is not the same. It has more luxuriant foliage, its colour is of a deeper and more purplish blue, and its corolla is wider in the mouth and flatter in the shape – a peculiarity which belongs to all the Italian campanulas, and distinguishes them from all others – while its roots are larger and thicker. Still, in spite of these differences, it is so like our own familiar flower, that it awoke a thrill of pleasant recognition in my heart, and gathered to itself a host of tender memories of far-off scenes.

FROM *THE RIVIERA* BY HUGH MACMILLAN (1833-1903)

Cheiranthus
WALLFLOWER

Fidelity in adversity

F lower in the crannied wall,
I pluck you out of the crannies;
Hold you here, root and all, in my hand,
Little flower – but if I could understand
What you are, root and all, and all in all,
I should know what God and man is.

ALFRED, LORD TENNYSON (1809-92)

1

2

3

4

5

6

7

8

9

10

11

12

13

14

15

Soon will the musk
carnations break and swell,
Soon will we have
gold-dusted snapdragon,
Sweet-William with his
homely cottage smell.

FROM *THYRSIS*
BY MATTHEW ARNOLD
(1822-1888)

20

21

22

23

16

24

17

25

18

26

19

27

28

29

30

31

*N*obody knows this
little Rose
It might a pilgrim be
Did I not take it from
the ways
And lift it up to thee.

EMILY DICKINSON
(1830-1886)

The Eglantine, a variety of wild rose, was widely planted in the early settlements in the United States because it grew quickly, could be clipped into a fragrant hedge and had a long life. In 1689, William Penn wrote to John Blackwell at Pennsbury: "Plow no more land than serves the house. Let the Gardiner, when come, take special care of getting quick setts and good speedy and quick shades… Let him plant wt. grows quickest, be sure woodbine and sweet brier, etc."

Legend has it that Penn took eighteen roses with him when he travelled from England to America for the second time.

A rose-bud by my early walk
Adown a corn-enclosed bawk
Sae gently bent its thorny stalk,
All on a dewy morning.

Ere twice the shades o' dawn are fled,
In a' its crimson glory spread
And drooping rich the dewy head,
It scents the early morning.

FROM *A ROSE-BUD BY MY EARLY WALK* BY
ROBERT BURNS (1759–96)

1

2

3

4

5

I saw the sweetest flower
wild nature yields,
A fresh blown musk-Rose.
'Twas the first that threw
Its sweets upon the summer;
graceful it grew
As is the wand that queen
Titania wields.
And, as I feasted on
its fragrancy,
I thought the garden-rose it
far excelled.

FROM
To a Friend who Sent me
Some Roses
BY JOHN KEATS
(1795-1821)

6

7

8

9

10

11

12

13

19

20

21

14

22

15

23

16

24

17

25

18

26

27

28

29

30

31

A rose, bent by the wind and pricked by thorns, yet has its heart turned upwards.

HUNA
(c. 216-297 AD)

LILIUM
WHITE LILY

Purity, Sweetness

There is not a flower in the garden again that groweth taller than the Lillie, reaching otherwhile to the height of three cubits from the ground: but a weak and slender neck it hath, and carries it not streight and upright, but it bendeth and noddeth downeward, as being not of strength sufficient to beare the weight of the head standing upon it. The flower is of incomparable whiteness, devided into leaves, without-forth are chamfered, narrow at the bottome, and by little and little spreading broader toward the top: fashioned all together in manner of a broad mouthed cup or beaker, the brims and lips whereof turne up somewhat backward round about and lie very open. Within these leaves there appeare certaine fine threads in manner of seeds: and just in the middest stand yellow chives, like as in Saffron.

FROM *THE NATURAL HISTORY* BY PLINY, TRANSLATED BY PHILEMON HOLLAND (1601)

FIELD LILY

Humility

Down in a meadow fresh and gay,
Picking lillies all the day;
Picking lillies both red and blue,
I little thought what love could do.

Where love is planted there it grows,
It buds and blossoms like any rose,
It has so sweet and a pleasant smell,
No flowers on earth can it excel.

TRADITIONAL RHYME

*R*ound the old walls observe
the ivy twine,
A plant attached to grandeur
in decline.
The tottering pile she grasps
in her embrace,
With a green mask conceals
its furrowed face,
And keeps it standing on its
time-worn base.

FROM *CHEPSTOW: A POEM*
BY EDWARD DAVIES
(1718-1789)

3

4

5

6

7

8

9

10

11

12

13

14

1

2

19

20

21

22

15

16

17

18

23

24

25

26

27

28

29

30

The Rose was sick and
smiling di'd;
And (being to be sanctifi'd)
About the Bed,
there sighing stood
The sweet, the flowrie
Sisterhood.

ROBERT HERRICK
(1591-1674)

"An October Garden"

*I*n my Autumn garden I was fain
To mourn among my scattered roses;
Alas for that lost rosebud that uncloses
To Autumn's languid sun and rain
When all the world is on the wane!
Which has not felt the sweet constraint of June,
Nor heard the nightingale in tune.

Broad-faced asters by my garden walk,
You are but coarse compared with roses:
More choice, more dear that rosebud which uncloses,
Faint-scented, pinched, upon its stalk,
That least and last which cold winds balk;
A rose it is though least and last of all,
A rose to me though at the fall.

Christina Rossetti (1830–94)

5

6

9

10

11

12

13

14

1

2

3

7

8

15

16

4

"*That's* right!" said the
Tiger-lily. "The daisies are
worst of all. When one speaks,
they all begin together, and it's
enough to make one wither to
hear the way they go on!"

FROM
Through the Looking Glass
by Lewis Carroll
(1832-1898)

17

18

19

20

21

22

23

24

25

26

27

28

29

30

31

A casement high and
triple-arched there was,
All garlanded with
Craven imag'ries.
Of fruits, and flowers, and
bunches of knot-grass.

FROM

THE EVE OF ST AGNES
BY JOHN KEATS
(1795-1821)

LILY-OF-THE-VALLEY

Return of happiness

A nd the naiad-like lily of the vale,
Whom youth makes so fair and passion so pale,
That the light of its tremulous bells is seen
Through their pavilions of tender green…

FROM *THE SENSITIVE PLANT* BY PERCY BYSSHE SHELLEY

(1792-1822)

CROCUS

Abuse not

Say, what impels, amidst surrounding snow
Congeal'd, the crocus' flamy bud to glow?
Say, what retards, amidst the summer's blaze,
Th' autumnal bulb, till pale, declining days?

The God of Seasons; whose pervading power
Controls the sun, or sheds the fleecy shower:
He bids each flower His quickening word obey,
Or to each lingering bloom enjoins delay.

FROM *THE NATURAL HISTORY OF SELBORNE* BY GILBERT WHITE (1720-93)

1

2

3

4

5

6

7

8

9

10

11

12

13

14

The rose, at edge of
winter now,
Doth fade with all its
summer glow;
Old are become the roses all,
Decline to age we also shall;
And with this prayer
I'll end my lay,
Amen, with me, O Parry say;
To us be rest from all annoy,
And a robust old age of joy.

FROM *THE INVITATION*
BY GORONWY OWEN
(1723-1769)

15

16

17

18

19

20

21

22

23

24

25

26

27

28

29

30

Love is like the wild
rose-briar;
Friendship like the holly-tree.
The holly is dark when the
rose-briar blooms,
But which will bloom
most constantly?

FROM *LOVE AND
FRIENDSHIP*
BY EMILY BRONTË
(1818-1848)

ANTIRRHINUM

SNAPDRAGON

Presumption

O h, how useful and beautiful are the tall yellow and the tall white Snapdragons! They can be played with in so many ways: potted up in the autumn, grown and flowered in a green house, cut back and planted out in the spring to flower again, admirable to send away; in fact, they have endless merits, and in a large clump in front of some dark corner or shrub they look very handsome indeed. They are lovely picked and on the dinner-table, especially the yellow Snapdragons, but, like many other things, they just want a little care and cultivation, which they often do not get; and they ought to be sown every April, and again in July.

FROM *POT-POURRI FROM A SURREY GARDEN* BY MRS C.W. EARLE

(1836–1925)

COLUMBINE

Folly

S till, still my eye will gaze long fixed on thee.

Till I forget that I am called a man,

And at thy side fast-rooted seem to be,

And the breeze comes my cheek with thine to fan.

Upon this craggy hill our life shall pass,

A life of summer days and summer joys,

Nodding our honey-bells mid pliant grass

In which the bee half-hid his time employs...

FROM *THE COLUMBINE* BY JONES VERY (1813–80)

1

2

3

4

5

6

7

8

9

10

11

12

13

14

15

16

17

The Michaelmas Daisies,
among dede weedes,
Bloom for St. Michael's
valorous deedes,
And seem the last of the
flowers that stoode
Till the feast of St. Simon
and St. Jude.

FROM *AN EARLY CALENDAR
OF ENGLISH FLOWERS*
ANON.

18

19

20

21

22

23

24

25

Althea with the purple eye;
the broom,
Yellow and bright as
bullion unalloyed
Her blossoms; and luxuriant
above all
The jasmine, throwing wide
her elegant sweets,
The deep dark green of whose
unvarnished leaf
Makes more conspicuous,
and illumines more
The bright profusion of her
scattered stars.

FROM *THE TASK*
BY WILLIAM COWPER
(1731-1800)

26

27

28

29

30

31

$\mathcal{I}$ said to the rose, "The brief night goes
In babble and revel and wine.
O young lord-lover, what sighs are those,
For one that will never be thine?
But mine, but mine," so I sware to the rose,
"For ever and ever, mine."

And the soul of the rose went into my blood,
As the music clash'd in the hall;
And long by the garden lake I stood,
For I heard your rivulet fall
From the lake to the meadow and on to the wood,
Our wood, that is dearer than all…

FROM *MAUD* BY ALFRED, LORD TENNYSON (1809–92)

BIRTHDAYS

JANUARY

1	17
2	18
3	19
4	20
5	21
6	22
7	23
8	24
9	25
10	26
11	27
12	28
13	29
14	30
15	31
16	

FEBRUARY·

1	17
2	18
3	19
4	20
5	21
6	22
7	23
8	24
9	25
10	26
11	27
12	28
13	29
14	
15	
16	

MARCH

1	17
2	18
3	19
4	20
5	21
6	22
7	23
8	24
9	25
10	26
11	27
12	28
13	29
14	30
15	31
16	

APRIL

1	17
2	18
3	19
4	20
5	21
6	22
7	23
8	24
9	25
10	26
11	27
12	28
13	29
14	30
15	
16	

MAY

1	17
2	18
3	19
4	20
5	21
6	22
7	23
8	24
9	25
10	26
11	27
12	28
13	29
14	30
15	31
16	

JUNE

1	17
2	18
3	19
4	20
5	21
6	22
7	23
8	24
9	25
10	26
11	27
12	28
13	29
14	30
15	
16	

B I R T H D A Y S

J U L Y

1		17	
2		18	
3		19	
4		20	
5		21	
6		22	
7		23	
8		24	
9		25	
10		26	
11		27	
12		28	
13		29	
14		30	
15		31	
16			

A U G U S T

1		17	
2		18	
3		19	
4		20	
5		21	
6		22	
7		23	
8		24	
9		25	
10		26	
11		27	
12		28	
13		29	
14		30	
15		31	
16			

S E P T E M B E R

1		17	
2		18	
3		19	
4		20	
5		21	
6		22	
7		23	
8		24	
9		25	
10		26	
11		27	
12		28	
13		29	
14		30	
15			
16			

O C T O B E R

1		17	
2		18	
3		19	
4		20	
5		21	
6		22	
7		23	
8		24	
9		25	
10		26	
11		27	
12		28	
13		29	
14		30	
15		31	
16			

N O V E M B E R

1		17	
2		18	
3		19	
4		20	
5		21	
6		22	
7		23	
8		24	
9		25	
10		26	
11		27	
12		28	
13		29	
14		30	
15			
16			

D E C E M B E R

1		17	
2		18	
3		19	
4		20	
5		21	
6		22	
7		23	
8		24	
9		25	
10		26	
11		27	
12		28	
13		29	
14		30	
15		31	
16			

IRIS
IRIS

Message

T hou art the iris, fair among the fairest,
  Who, armed with golden rod
And winged with the celestial azure, bearest
The message of some God.

Thou art the Muse, who far from crowded cities,
Hauntest the sylvan streams,
Playing on pipes of reed the artless ditties
That come to us as dreams.

FROM *FLOWER-DE-LUCE* BY HENRY WADSWORTH

LONGFELLOW (1807-82)

YEAR PLANNER

JANUARY

1 ....   17 ....
2 ....   18 ....
3 ....   19 ....
4 ....   20 ....
5 ....   21 ....
6 ....   22 ....
7 ....   23 ....
8 ....   24 ....
9 ....   25 ....
10 ....   26 ....
11 ....   27 ....
12 ....   28 ....
13 ....   29 ....
14 ....   30 ....
15 ....   31 ....
16 ....

FEBRUARY

1 ....   17 ....
2 ....   18 ....
3 ....   19 ....
4 ....   20 ....
5 ....   21 ....
6 ....   22 ....
7 ....   23 ....
8 ....   24 ....
9 ....   25 ....
10 ....   26 ....
11 ....   27 ....
12 ....   28 ....
13 ....   29 ....
14 ....
15 ....
16 ....

MARCH

1 ....   17 ....
2 ....   18 ....
3 ....   19 ....
4 ....   20 ....
5 ....   21 ....
6 ....   22 ....
7 ....   23 ....
8 ....   24 ....
9 ....   25 ....
10 ....   26 ....
11 ....   27 ....
12 ....   28 ....
13 ....   29 ....
14 ....   30 ....
15 ....   31 ....
16 ....

APRIL

1 ....   17 ....
2 ....   18 ....
3 ....   19 ....
4 ....   20 ....
5 ....   21 ....
6 ....   22 ....
7 ....   23 ....
8 ....   24 ....
9 ....   25 ....
10 ....   26 ....
11 ....   27 ....
12 ....   28 ....
13 ....   29 ....
14 ....   30 ....
15 ....
16 ....

MAY

1 ....   17 ....
2 ....   18 ....
3 ....   19 ....
4 ....   20 ....
5 ....   21 ....
6 ....   22 ....
7 ....   23 ....
8 ....   24 ....
9 ....   25 ....
10 ....   26 ....
11 ....   27 ....
12 ....   28 ....
13 ....   29 ....
14 ....   30 ....
15 ....   31 ....
16 ....

JUNE

1 ....   17 ....
2 ....   18 ....
3 ....   19 ....
4 ....   20 ....
5 ....   21 ....
6 ....   22 ....
7 ....   23 ....
8 ....   24 ....
9 ....   25 ....
10 ....   26 ....
11 ....   27 ....
12 ....   28 ....
13 ....   29 ....
14 ....   30 ....
15 ....
16 ....

YEAR PLANNER

JULY

1	17
2	18
3	19
4	20
5	21
6	22
7	23
8	24
9	25
10	26
11	27
12	28
13	29
14	30
15	31
16	

AUGUST

1	17
2	18
3	19
4	20
5	21
6	22
7	23
8	24
9	25
10	26
11	27
12	28
13	29
14	30
15	31
16	

SEPTEMBER

1	17
2	18
3	19
4	20
5	21
6	22
7	23
8	24
9	25
10	26
11	27
12	28
13	29
14	30
15	
16	

OCTOBER

1	17
2	18
3	19
4	20
5	21
6	22
7	23
8	24
9	25
10	26
11	27
12	28
13	29
14	30
15	31
16	

NOVEMBER

1	17
2	18
3	19
4	20
5	21
6	22
7	23
8	24
9	25
10	26
11	27
12	28
13	29
14	30
15	
16	

DECEMBER

1	17
2	18
3	19
4	20
5	21
6	22
7	23
8	24
9	25
10	26
11	27
12	28
13	29
14	30
15	31
16	

"SONG"

Weep, as if you thought of laughter!
Smile, as tears were coming after!
Marry your pleasures to your woes;
And think life's green well worth its rose!

No sorrow will your heart betide,
Without a comfort by its side;
The sun may sleep in his sea-bed,
But you have starlight overhead.

Trust not to Joy! the rose of June,
When opened wide, will wither soon;
Italian days without twilight
Will turn them suddenly to night.

Joy, most changeful of all things,
Flits away on rainbow wings;
And when they look the gayest know
It is that they are spread to go!

ELIZABETH BARRETT BROWNING (1806–61)

ACKNOWLEDGEMENTS

The Publishers would like to thank the picture libraries below for permission to reproduce the following paintings in this book:

Fine Art Photographic: p2 Eloise Harriet Stannard, *A Still Life of Chrysanthemums*, Burlington Paintings; p7 Mabel Ashby, *A Blooming Relationship, A Rosy Future*; p10: Basel Besler, *Clematis Coerulea Pannonica*, Trowbridge Gallery; p11 Emile Faivre, *A Still Life of Clematis*; p14/15 Luigi Maggiorani, *Elegant Ladies Gathering Roses*, Galerie Berko; p19 Anonymous, *A Poppy Basket*, Private Collection; p22/3 Henry John Yeend King, *Cottage Gardeners*; p26 Anonymous, *The Wedding*; p27: Vittorio Reggianini, *La Rose*, Gelerie Berko; p34 Herman Seeger, *Summer's Delight*, Anthony Mitchell Paintings; p35 William Kay Blacklock, *Gathering Wild Flowers*; p38 Walter Crane, *The Garden*; p43 Robert Gordon, *Pruning Roses*; p50 Thomas Worsey, *Still Life of Foxgloves, Mushrooms, Snapdragons and Thistles*, Anthony Mitchell Fine Paintings; p54/55 Abbey Altson, *An Arabian Fantasy*, Baumkotter Gallery; p58 Alfred Godchauz, *A Still Life of Iris and Roses*, Gaving Graham;

Visual Arts Library: p18 Augusta Laessoe, *Wild Roses, Poppies and Maguerites*; p46 Emma Loffler, *Blossom and Lily-of-the-Valley*; p47 Johan Lurentz Jensen, *Crocus on a Table*; p59 John Jesssop Hardwick, *Iris and Christmas Rose*, Chris Beetles Gallery; p62 Auguste Renoir, *Roses by the Window.*